The Science of Living Things

What is a Whale?

Bobbie Kalman & Heather Levigne

Crabtree Publishing Company

www.Crabtreebooks.com

The Science of Living Things Series
A Bobbie Kalman Book

**For my friend Karuna Thal,
who swims with dolphins and whales**

Editor-in-Chief
Bobbie Kalman

Writing team
Bobbie Kalman
Heather Levigne

Managing editor
Lynda Hale

Editors
Niki Walker
Hannelore Sotzek

Copy Editor
Kate Calder

Computer design
Lynda Hale
Trevor Morgan (cover type)

**Production coordinator
and photo researcher**
Hannelore Sotzek

Consultant
Cynthia D'Vincent,
Intersea Foundation, California

Special thanks to
Kina Scudi, SeaWorld San Diego; Karuna Thal, for sharing her dolphin stories

Photographs
Frank Balthis: page 25 (bottom); Tom Campbell's Photographic/ © Peter C. Howorth: front cover, pages 9, 24; Tom Campbell's Photographic/© Doug Perrine: pages 3, 8, 19; Digital Stock: back cover; Cynthia D'Vincent/Intersea Foundation: title page, pages 23, 26, 31; Jeff Foott/Tom Stack & Associates: pages 11, 14-15, 16; Bobbie Kalman: page 5; Thomas Kitchin/Tom Stack & Associates: page 22; Flip Nicklin/First Light: page 17; Sea World, Inc./Ken Bohn: page 18; Sea World, Inc./Bobbie Kalman: pages 4, 25 (top); Douglas David Seifert/EarthWater: pages 20-21; Dave Watts/Tom Stack & Associates: page 30

Illustrations
Barbara Bedell: pages 6-7, 10 (bottom), 11, 13 (top), 15, 16, 17, 18, 27, 28, 29
Karen Harrison: pages 12, 13 (bottom)
Jeannette McNaughton-Julich: pages 5, 20, 23
Trevor Morgan: page 10 (top)

Separations and film
Dot 'n Line Image Inc.

Printer
Worzalla Publishing Company

Crabtree Publishing Company

PMB 16A
350 Fifth Ave.,
Suite 3308
N.Y., N.Y. 10118

612 Welland Ave.,
St. Catharines,
Ontario, Canada
L2M 5V6

73 Lime Walk
Headington
Oxford OX3 7AD
United Kingdom

Cataloging in Publication Data
Kalman, Bobbie
    What is a whale?

(The science of living things)
Includes index.

ISBN 0-86505-935-7 (library bound) ISBN 0-86505-953-5 (pbk.)
This book introduces the physiology, habitats, feeding, and behavior of different types of whales and discusses whale watching.

1. Whales—Juvenile literature. [1. Whales.] I. Levigne, Heather.
II. Title. III. Series: Kalman, Bobbie. Science of living things.

QL737.C4 K255   j599.5 21   LC 99-30370
                                                              CIP

Contents

What is a whale?

*Although whales spend all their time in water, they do not have **gills** for breathing underwater as fish do. The beluga shown above is coming to the surface of the water to breathe air.*

Whales belong to a group of animals called **cetaceans**. Cetaceans are **mammals**. They are **warm-blooded** animals, which means their body can adjust so that its temperature stays the same in hot or cold surroundings. Like all mammals, whales breathe **oxygen** to survive. Unlike other animals, female mammals can make milk in their body to feed their babies.

Whales need water

Whales are **marine** mammals. They spend their entire life in salt water. Water helps support the weight of their body. A whale's body weight is so great that its lungs and other organs would be crushed if it were on land. Whales also need water to keep their skin moist. Without water, their skin dries out and their body overheats. If a whale becomes stranded on a beach for a long period of time, it will die.

Where do whales live?

Whales live in oceans all over the world, from warm, tropical waters to icy polar regions. Many whales move from one place to another to feed or **mate**. River dolphins are the only cetaceans that live in freshwater **habitats**, or homes. They live in deep, muddy rivers.

Dolphins are related to whales. Like all cetaceans, dolphins live in water and need to keep their skin moist.

Ancient ancestor

Whales are descended from a fur-covered, four-legged mammal that lived on land millions of years ago. This mammal often waded into shallow water to find food. As it spent more time in the water, it **evolved**, or gradually changed over time. Its fur disappeared, paddle-like flippers replaced its front legs, and its back legs became smaller until they disappeared. The nostrils of this land ancestor moved to the top of its head and became a **blowhole**.

The whale family tree

There are 76 **species**, or types, of whales. Scientists divide them into two major groups—**baleen** and **toothed** whales.

Baleen whales

Baleen whales are the largest whales. Their Latin name is *mysticetes*, which means "mustached" and refers to their bristly baleen.

*Humpback whales have the largest **pectoral fins**, or flippers.*

Gray whales have many bumps, scratches, and scars on their skin.

Right whales swim with their mouth open.

Scientists think that the blue whale is the largest animal that has ever lived on Earth.

Toothed whales

Dolphins and porpoises
are some of the 66 species
of toothed whales.

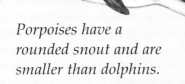

*Porpoises have a
rounded snout and are
smaller than dolphins.*

*There are more than
26 kinds of dolphins.*

*Orcas belong
to the dolphin
family. They are
the only dolphins
that eat warm-
blooded animals.*

*Sperm whales
are the largest
toothed whales.*

*Can you guess how the
beaked whale got its name?*

*The name beluga comes from a
Russian word meaning "white."*

*The narwhal is known as the
"unicorn of the sea."*

Flukes, fins, and blowholes

A whale's body is designed for living in water. It is **fusiform**, or torpedo-shaped, and has smooth, rubbery skin that helps the whale glide easily through water.

*A thick layer of **blubber**, or fat, traps the whale's body heat and helps keep the animal warm in cold water.*

Whales have no sense of smell.

***Flippers** help a whale steer through water.*

Whales have excellent hearing. They can hear for miles underwater.

*A whale's tail has two **flukes**. Whales move their flukes up and down to help push their body through the water.*

How do whales breathe?

Mammals inhale oxygen from the air. They exhale **carbon dioxide**. When other mammals hold their breath, they need to exhale after a short time because carbon dioxide builds up in their body and must be released quickly. A whale can hold its breath for a long time because carbon dioxide does not build up as quickly in its body.

Oxygen in the body

Blood carries oxygen throughout an animal's body. Whales have more blood in their body than other types of mammals do. More blood allows them to store more oxygen. Having great amounts of oxygen in their body allows whales to remain underwater for long periods of time before surfacing for fresh air.

A whale breathes through its blowhole. When it dives, it closes the hole to keep out water. Toothed whales have a single blowhole, but baleen whales have two.

To breathe while swimming, a whale curves its body at the water's surface to expose its blowhole.

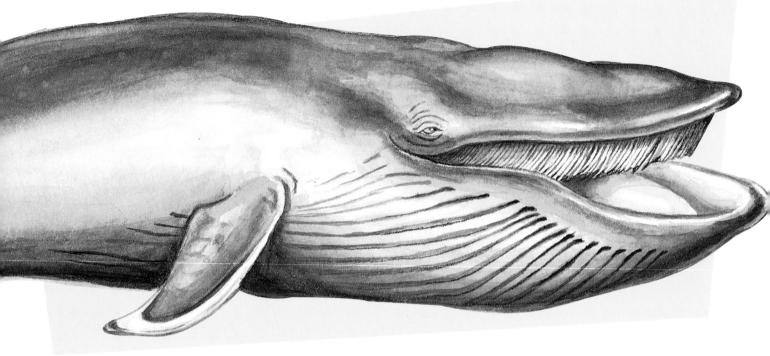

Baleen whales

There are two groups of baleen whales: **right whales** and **rorquals**. Most baleen whales are larger than toothed whales. They travel alone or in small groups.

Bristles instead of teeth

Baleen whales do not have teeth for grasping or chewing food. They use baleen plates to catch their food. The plates hang in the whale's mouth like the bristles of a broom. They are made from **keratin**—the same material as that found in fingernails. The baleen of some whales is longer than that of others.

To feed, a whale takes in a huge mouthful of water and pushes it out through its baleen with its tongue. The baleen plates trap tiny **crustaceans** called **krill**, which the whale then swallows. Krill are only 2 inches (5 cm) long. In order to get enough energy for its huge body, a whale eats several tons of krill every day. Baleen also traps small fish such as herring, which the whales swallow whole.

krill

Bottom-feeders

Gray whales are **bottom-feeders**. They dive deep in order to find crustaceans buried in the muddy ocean floor. Using their snout, gray whales stir up the mud and suck food into their mouth, filtering out the muddy water through their short baleen. **Barnacles** and whale lice cluster on the skin of gray whales. Barnacles are crustaceans that cement themselves onto the face, flippers, and flukes of some large sea creatures.

Most gray whales suck food through the right side of their mouth, wearing down the baleen on that side.

*To trap fish, humpback whales often use **cooperative feeding**. They swim below a school of fish and make high-pitched sounds that frighten the fish into a tight group. The whales **bubble-net**, or blow bubbles that form a "net" around the school, trapping the fish long enough for the humpbacks to rise and swallow them.*

Right whales

Northern right whales, southern right whales, and bowhead whales make up the group of whales called **right whales**. These whales have a huge head, long baleen, and a thick layer of blubber. They have no **dorsal**, or back, fin. Their head is covered with rough patches of skin called **callosities**. Scientists are able to identify individual whales by the pattern of their callosities.

Bowhead whales

A bowhead whale's baleen is longer than that of any other whale. Its baleen is up to thirteen feet (4 m) long. Unlike other right whales, bowheads have no callosities. These smooth black whales live in the cold waters of the Arctic.

(above) Right whales such as this bowhead were named by whalers who considered them the "right" whales to hunt because they were easy to catch.

The whale hunters

In the past, whalers hunted right whales for baleen. Baleen is strong and bends easily. It was used to make fishing rods, springs for carriages, and undergarments called **corsets**. Women wore corsets to look thin. Before people used electricity, blubber was melted and burned as fuel in oil lamps. The whalers also sold whale meat and skin. Whale hunting killed thousands of whales. It was a dangerous job, as shown below, but the whalers still did it because it paid well.

The long ribs in corsets were made of whalebone, or baleen.

Rorquals

Humpback, blue, fin, sei, minke, and Bryde's whales are rorquals. The largest and fastest species of whales belong to this group. Rorquals are the only whales that have grooves on their throat called **ventral pleats**. The pleats expand when the whales feed and allow them to take in huge mouthfuls of water. The name rorqual comes from a Norwegian word meaning "ruby-throated." When a rorqual takes a big gulp of water, its ventral pleats stretch, and its throat turns red or pink.

Humpback whales

Humpback whales, shown left, are studied more than most whale species. They are named for the way they dive. Just before they go underwater, they arch their back. Their arched back makes their body appear humpbacked.

Toothed whales

Toothed whales include sperm whales, belugas, beaked whales, narwhals, dolphins, and porpoises. They have sharp teeth for catching fish. Orcas can go onto land to catch seals, as shown in the picture above. Most toothed whales travel in groups called **pods**. Scientists think that the members of a pod whistle to one another to share information about the location of food and predators. They stay close together for protection and hunt as a group.

Belugas

Belugas are also called white whales. When they are born, their body is dark gray. As they grow into adults, they turn blue and then white. A beluga's neck is flexible, allowing it to turn its head from side to side. Most other whales can look only straight ahead. Belugas live in the Arctic Ocean where ice covers part of the water's surface. They breathe air trapped in pockets under the ice or break holes in the ice with their head so they can breathe.

Sperm whales

Sperm whales are the largest of the toothed whales. They are named for the **spermaceti** organ inside their head. This organ is filled with oil that helps the whale float near the surface of the water. When a sperm whale makes a deep dive, the cold water causes the oil to become solid and heavy, helping the whale stay down.

Narwhals

Narwhals have only two teeth, both of which are located on their upper jaw. These whales prey on fish, crabs, shrimp, and squid. Narwhals cannot chew their food so they swallow it whole. One of a male narwhal's teeth grows into a long **tusk**. Only a few have two tusks. Most female narwhals do not grow tusks at all.

During mating season, male narwhals have "sword fights" with their tusks. They compete with other males for the right to mate with a female.

Dolphins and porpoises

Dolphins and porpoises are the smallest of the toothed whales. They are excellent swimmers and jumpers! Most species live in large pods. Dolphins often hunt in groups of up to a thousand animals. The dolphins surround a school of fish and then take turns charging into the school to feed. They also follow fishing boats and eat fish that are stirred up by fishing nets.

Orcas

Orcas, shown below, are the largest dolphins. They are also known as killer whales because they are excellent hunters. There are two types of orcas. **Resident** orcas live in small groups in a small area of the ocean and eat mainly fish. **Transient** orcas travel in larger groups and eat squid, fish, sea lions, as well as other whales and dolphins.

Bottlenosed dolphins spend much of their time swimming, leaping, and hunting. To rest, cetaceans do not sleep as other mammals do. They rest near the surface of the water and rise to take a breath every few minutes.

Baby whales

Mammals give birth to **live young**. Live young are babies that do not hatch from eggs. A mother whale is called a **cow**. Every two or three years, a cow gives birth to a **calf**, or baby whale. Unlike most mammals, whales are born tailfirst. When a calf is born, its mother pushes it to the surface of the water so it can breathe. Calves know how to swim as soon as they are born. They stay with their mother for several months. They ride along in her **slipstream**, or the waves created by her body movements, until they are strong enough to swim alone.

Drink your milk!

Baby whales **nurse**, or drink milk from their mother's body. Calves nurse several times a day for short periods of time because they need to go to the surface often to breathe.

Cows have two openings on their body called **mammary slits**. Inside each slit is a nipple. To nurse, a calf curls its tongue around the nipple, forming a tube. The mother squirts milk into the calf's mouth through this tube.

The drawing on the right shows a spinner dolphin calf nursing. The sperm whale calves in the photograph are riding along in the female whale's slipstream.

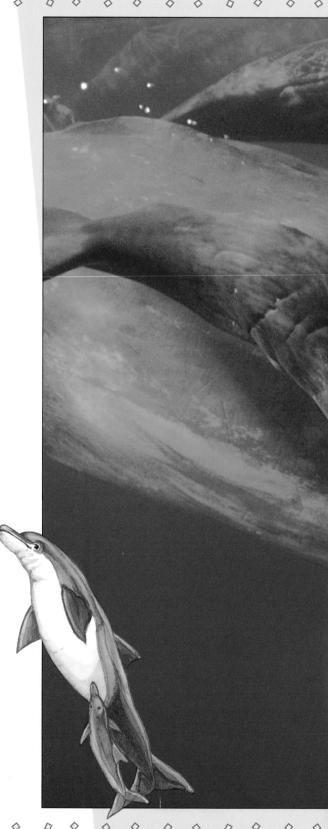

How whales communicate

Whales **communicate**, or send messages to one another, in many ways. Sound and touch are two important types of communication. Whales that live in groups communicate more than those that live alone or in pairs.

Showing affection

Whales nuzzle and rub their bodies against one another to show affection. Humpbacks use their long flippers to touch other whales in their group. Some whales also seem to enjoy being rubbed and patted by people.

Wailing whales

Male humpback whales sing songs during their mating period. All the whales in a winter feeding ground sing the same song, which is different from the songs of humpback whales in other areas. A whale's song is made up of a series of squeaks, moans, chirps, and sighs. Scientists think that the whales may sing to attract females and warn other males to stay away.

*This orca is **lobtailing**, or raising its flukes out of the water and slapping them against the surface. The noise may send a message to other whales.*

Singing for their supper

Humpback whales, which hunt and feed in groups, use sound to help catch the fish. One or two whales lead the pod. One whale sings a feeding song, which frightens fish that the pod is hunting into a tight group. The entire pod lunges through the water, scooping up mouthfuls of food as shown below. After whales have hunted together a number of times, each member of the pod performs its specific task each time the group hunts.

Some toothed whales use **echolocation** to find objects underwater. They send out sounds from the **nasal sacs** inside their head. These sounds hit objects in the water and bounce back to the whale as echoes. The whale can tell by the echoes whether the object nearby is food, an enemy, or other animals.

Humpback whales often return to the same group to feed. After repeating their technique several times, they seem to work well together, which enables them to catch more fish.

Why do whales do that?

Marine biologists are scientists who study whales in their natural habitat. They take photographs of them and gather information about their behavior. In order to study whales, scientists identify them by the color patterns on the underside of their flukes. Studying whales helps scientists develop **theories**, or ideas, about why whales do certain things.

Jumping for joy?

Whales often **breach**, or leap into the air and then crash onto the surface of the water, landing on their side or back. There are many reasons for breaching. Whales that are surprised by people in their habitat sometimes breach. They may breach to show fear or anger. Some scientists think breaching is a playful activity and that the whales do it just for fun!

Flipping out

Humpback whales have longer flippers than whales of other species. They often wave their flippers in the air or slap them on the surface of the water. Some scientists think that this behavior, called **pectoral fin-slapping**, or **pec-slapping**, helps scare away predators that might attack baby whales. Whales often pec-slap for no apparent reason, however.

Of all the whale species, dolphins are among the most playful.

*Whales **spyhop**, or stick their head out of the water, in order to look around above the surface.*

Whale watching

Whales **migrate**, or move, thousands of miles every year between their feeding and breeding grounds. In summer they live in cold water; in winter they move to warmer water. They often return to the same places each time.

Cold water has more oxygen than warm water. Living things need oxygen to survive, so many sea creatures live in cold water. Whales spend the summer eating large amounts of food in their cold-water feeding grounds to prepare for their migration to warm water, where there is less food.

Scientists think that whales migrate to warmer water before giving birth because the water in their feeding grounds is too cold and rough for newborn calves. When the babies are strong enough, the whales return to colder oceans to feed.

Many people come to watch whales as they migrate. Watching whales can be fun, but it is important that the boats stay a safe distance away from the whales. Too many boats disturb the whales and can separate the mothers from their calves.

Whale watching in Hawaii

In April I was on the island of Kauai, a Hawaiian island. From my balcony overlooking the Pacific Ocean, I could see humpback whales swimming by all day long. You can spot a whale by the puff of mist rising out of its blowhole. Some of the whales were far out in the ocean, but many swam close to shore in the shallower waters. I noticed their huge pectoral fins stick out and slap the water. I imagined that they were waving at me and decided to get closer to them. A few days later I went on a whale-watching cruise. The captain told us that, for the safety of the humpbacks, boats were not allowed to go within 100 yards (92 m) of a pod, but that the whales often swam closer to the boats.

The boat stopped each time there was a whale sighting. The captain announced that there was a pod of humpback whales nearby. Everyone ran to the railings to have a look. The whales swam slowly towards us. Everyone on the boat was awed by the enormous mammals. They were far bigger than I ever imagined they would be! There were loud whooshing noises as the whales exhaled from their blowholes. One of the mothers pushed her calf out of the water. I thought to myself, "She's showing us her baby!"

Surrounded by dolphins

On our way home, there were over a hundred spinner dolphins around our boat. They put on a spectacular show—leaping out of the water and spinning high in the air. We waved at them and clapped, thoroughly enjoying the entertainment. They accompanied us for miles, swimming under and beside our boat.

Dancing with the dolphins

The next day, I was playing loud music and dancing around my balcony. I was feeling happy about seeing the whales and dolphins the day before! As I looked out over the ocean, I saw a group of dolphins spinning and leaping along with me. I shouted to them, "Do you like my music?" Do you think they did?

Dolphin friends

My friend Karuna lives in Kauai and swims with the dolphins almost every day. She paddles far out into the ocean in her kayak, glides quietly into the water, and then starts singing "dolphin songs." When the dolphins hear her singing, they often come and swim with her. Here is one of her stories.

The 21-dolphin salute

"One day, when I entered the water, I could hear many dolphin voices clicking and squeaking. There were four or five pods of 12 to 20 dolphins in the bay. They were playing in different ways. Some swam belly to belly and leapt out of the water, spinning. Several were just a few days old. I called to them, clapped my hands, and shouted, 'Good job!' Suddenly, they dove under. For a moment, all was quiet, and then a whole long line of dolphins leapt out of the water at the same time. I called that show the 21-dolphin salute. I believed it was the dolphins' way of saying goodbye to me."

Whales in danger

In the past, whalers killed thousands of whales, and many species became **endangered**, or in danger of becoming **extinct**. Whale hunting is still legal in some countries, but the whalers are limited to the number of whales that they are allowed to hunt. Some whalers still kill more whales than they are allowed, however. Pollution also kills many whales; fishing nets trap dolphins, causing them to drown.

Protecting whales

Organizations such as the International Whaling Commission are helping protect whales in their natural habitat. In 1974, the Marine Mammal Protection Act was created to help protect whales and other marine mammals from being over-hunted. Efforts such as these have saved some whale species, including gray whales, which are no longer considered endangered.

These pilot whales are stranded on a beach in Australia. Scientists are not sure why whales strand.

Words to know

baleen Long bristles in a whale's mouth used for filtering food from water

bubble-netting A whale's action of catching food by trapping small fish in a net of bubbles

callosity Rough skin on a whale's body

carbon dioxide A gas, made up of carbon and oxygen, that is present in air

cooperative feeding Working together in a group to catch food

crustacean An animal that has a hard shell and a jointed body and legs

extinct Describing a plant or animal that no longer exists

gill A body part used by a fish for breathing underwater

lobtailing A whale's action of slapping the surface of the water with its flukes

nasal sac A hollow organ in a dolphin's head that is used to make sounds for echolocation

oxygen A gas present in air that humans, animals, and plants need to breathe

pectoral-fin slapping A whale's action of raising its flippers and slapping them on the surface of the water

spyhop A whale's action of raising its head out of the water

Index

4 5 6 7 8 9 0 Printed in the U.S.A. 8 7 6 5 4 3 2